KETO DESSERTS COOKBOOK

The Ultimate Keto Desserts Meal Plan
Guideto Fill your Sweet Cravings and
the Secret Formula to Lose Excessive
Weight at the Same Time –A Priceless
Gift for Ketogenic Diet Beginners

Table of Contents

INTRODUCTION

A keto dessert is one that is high in fat, moderate in protein, and low in carbs. Regular ingredients for keto desserts incorporate:

- almond flour and coconut flour

- coconut cream/full-fat coconut milk

- hefty whipping cream

- full fat cream cheddar, ideally refined

- nuts or seeds, ideally drenched or grew

- berries, cranberries, lemon, and lime

- cacao powder, cocoa spread, and stevia-improved chocolate chips

- unsweetened, shredded coconut

- almond, nut, and walnut spreads

- eggs

- fats like margarine, ghee, coconut oil, and avocado oil.

Keto desserts are additionally separate in that they don't contain grains or grain-based flours or any type of sugar, regardless of whether white sugar or an entire sugar like nectar or maple syrup. Keto desserts are supplementing thick in light of their emphasis on sound fats, quality protein, and no sugar. Those are the chomps that tally, regardless of whether they're dessert

Keto Dessert Recipes

35+ recipes

1. Keto Molten Lava Cake

Prep Time: 10 min |Cook Time: 15 min | Total Time: 25 min

Ingredients

- 1 tablespoon Almond flour
- 2 tablespoon Unsalted Butter softened
- 2 large eggs at room temperature
- ¼ cup Unsweetened cocoa powder

- 3 tablespoon Swerve confectioners sugar substitute
- ½ teaspoon Baking powder
- ½ teaspoon Vanilla concentrate

Guidelines

1. Preheat the oven to 350°F degrees.
2. In a blending bowl, join the ingredients together and beat on high until smooth and rich.
3. Empty the hitter equitably into two all around lubed 6-ounce ramekins.
4. Prepare for 12-15 minutes, or until the edges of the cake are firm, however the middle actually has a little wiggle to it.
5. Let cool for a few minutes, and afterward turn over onto a plate to serve.
6. Topping with sugar free whipped cream whenever wanted.

2. Keto baked Pumpkin Muffins

Preparation Time: 14-Mins | Cooking Time: 5-Mins | Serving: 5

INGREDIENTS

- 1 1/2 cups of flour
- 3/4 cup sugar
- 1 tsp baking powder
- 1-teaspoon of baking powder
- 1/4 teaspoon of salt
- 1-teaspoon pumpkin pie spice
- 1 1/2 cups pumpkin puree
- 1/4 cup butter, melted/cooled
- 1-teaspoon of vanilla extract

- 1-egg
- 4 oz cream cheese, softened
- 1/2 teaspoon vanilla extract
- 1-teaspoon of flour
- 2 tbsp sugar
- 1-teaspoon of milk

DIRECTIONS

1. Preheat the oven to 350 stages and line a muffin tray with liners or cooking spray.
2. In a large bowl, add the flour, sugar, baking powder, baking powder, salt, and pumpkin spice.
3. Place pumpkin, melted butter, vanilla extract, and egg in a separate bowl
4. Combine the wet mixture with the dry aggregate and stir until simply combined.
5. Fill muffin liners with batter about three / four full.
6. To make cream cheese filling: Put all substances in a bowl and integrate.
7. Using a play bag or layer with a different tip out and a dollop, what can you put in the

muffin cups. * It will sink almost completely.

8.   Place the muffin tray in an oven to bake for about 18-20 minutes.

9.   Remove from oven and let cool for 2-3 minutes before discarding.

3. Keto Classic Cheesecake

Preparation Time: 10-Mins | Cooking Time: 5-Mins | Serving: 2

INGREDIENTS

- 1 1/2 cups Graham cracker crumbs
- 1/4 teaspoon ground cinnamon
- 1/3 cup unsalted butter or margarine, mixed
- 4 (8 oz.) Packets of cream cheese, softened
- 1 1/4 cups of sugar
- 1/2 cup of sour cream
- 2-teaspoons vanilla extract

- 5-large eggs
- 1/2 cup of sour cream
- 2-teaspoons of sugar

DIRECTIONS

1. Preheat the whole thing to 475 ° F. Place a pan crammed with half the water in oven.

2. Made crust: Mix graham cracker crumbs and cinnamon; add butter or margarine. It is placed on the bottom and 2/3 of the man, a 9-piece springform pan chosen with parchment. Take a large portion of the entire bottom of the pan. Release until completion is complete.

3. Make the following: Use an electric mixer to avoid a different, bitter and bitter taste. Blend until smooth and creamy. Scrape off parts of the bottle. View the dishes in a bowl; And get a new dimension. But not until things are known.

4. Remove something from ourselves and get to work. There is certainly a good choice in a bath. BAK for 12 minutes; turn to 350 ° F once and bake until top of procedure turns golden, 50 to 60 minutes. Remove something to a rack to choose from.

5. Make the following: Combine our cream and sugar; Undo. Care for and refrigerate in less than four hours.

4.   Keto Cracker Barrel's Double Fudge Coca Cola Chocolate Cake

Preparation Time: 14-Mins | Cooking Time: 5-Mins | Serving: 5

INGREDIENTS

- 1 cup of coca-cola
- 1/2 cup of vegetable oil
- 1/2 cup (1 stick) salted butter
- 3-heaped tablespoons of dark cocoa powder
- 2 cups of granulated sugar
- 2 cups of All-purpose Flour
- 2-large eggs
- 1/2 cup of buttermilk
- 1-teaspoon of baking powder

- 1-teaspoon of vanilla extract
- 1-stick of salted butter
- 3-tablespoons of dark cocoa powder
- 6-tablespoons of milk
- 1-teaspoon of vanilla extract
- 4 cups of powdered sugar

DIRECTIONS

1. Preheat the oven to 350 ° F.
2. Butter and flour a 9x13 pan and set aside.
3. Stir sugar and flour in a large bowl of a mixer and set aside.
4. Bring cola, oil, butter, and cocoa to the boil in a pan. Pour into the flour combination and beat on about medium-low until a toothpick inserted in the center comes out clean, immediately after removing the cake from the oven, along with frosting.

5. In a saucepan, bring butter, cocoa powder, and milk to a boil over medium heat. Remove from heat and whisk in icing sugar and vanilla. Pour over cake and quickly unfold. Let the cake cool to room temperature, then put it in the fridge until served.

5.   Pineapple Carrot Cake

Total Time: 1 hr. | Prep: 20 min. Bake: 35 min. + cooling | Makes: 12 servings

Ingredients

- 2 cups all-purpose flour
- 2 cups sugar
- 2 teaspoons preparing pop
- 2 teaspoons ground cinnamon
- 1 teaspoon salt
- 1-1/2 cups canola oil
- 4 huge eggs, room temperature
- 3 containers (4 ounces each) carrot child food
- 1 can (8 ounces) squashed pineapple, depleted
- 1/2 cup chopped pecans
- Icing:

- 1 bundle (8 ounces) cream cheddar, relaxed
- 1/2 cup margarine, relaxed
- 1 teaspoon vanilla concentrate
- 3-3/4 cups confectioners' sugar
- Extra chopped pecans and palatable blooms, discretionary

Directions

1. In a bowl, join the dry ingredients. Add the oil, eggs and infant food; blend on low speed until all around mixed. Mix in pineapple and nuts. Fill 2 lubed and floured 9-in. round preparing dish. Heat at 350° until a toothpick embedded in the middle confesses all, 35-40 minutes. Cool for 10 minutes prior to eliminating from skillet to wire racks to cool totally.

2. For icing, in a bowl, beat cream cheddar and margarine until smooth. Beat in vanilla and confectioners' sugar until combination arrives at spreading consistency. Spread among layers and up and over and sides of cake. Trimming with nuts and blooms whenever wanted. Store in the cooler.

6. Triple-Chocolate Cheesecake Bars

Prep: 35 min. Bake: 25 min. + chilling | Makes: 2-1/2 dozen

Ingredients

- 1/4 cup spread, cubed
- 1/2 cup sugar
- 3 tablespoons heating cocoa
- 1/2 teaspoon vanilla concentrate
- 1 enormous egg, room temperature
- 1/4 cup all-purpose flour
- 1/8 teaspoon heating powder
- 1/8 teaspoon salt

CHEESECAKE LAYER:

- 2 bundles (8 ounces each) cream cheddar, relaxed

- 1/2 cup sugar
- 1-1/2 teaspoons vanilla concentrate
- 3/4 cup semisweet chocolate chips, liquefied and cooled
- 2 enormous eggs, room temperature, daintily beaten

GANACHE:
- 1-1/2 cups semisweet chocolate chips
- 1/2 cup weighty whipping cream
- 1 teaspoon vanilla concentrate

Directions

1. Preheat oven to 350°. Line a 13x9-in. skillet with foil, allowing finishes to reach out up sides; oil foil. In a microwave, dissolve margarine in an enormous microwave-safe bowl. Mix in sugar, cocoa and vanilla. Add egg; mix well. Add flour, heating powder and salt; mix just until consolidated. Spread as a far layer in arranged skillet. Heat until top seems dry, 6-8 minutes.

2. In the interim, in a huge bowl, beat cream cheddar, sugar and vanilla until smooth. Beat in cooled chocolate chips. Add beaten eggs; beat on low speed just until

consolidated. Spread over brownie layer. Heat until filling is set, 25-30 minutes. Cool 10 minutes on a wire rack.

3. For ganache, place chocolate contributes a small bowl. In a pot, heat cream just to the point of boiling. Pour over chocolate; let stand 5 minutes. Mix with a rush until smooth. Mix in vanilla; cool marginally, mixing occasionally. Pour over cheesecake layer; cool in container on a wire rack 60 minutes. Refrigerate at any rate 2 hours. Lifting with foil, eliminate brownies from dish. Cut into bars.

7.   Cookie Butter Pie

Prep: 20 min. + freezing | Makes: 2 pies (8 servings each)

Ingredients

- 1 package (8 ounces) cream cheese, softened
- 1 cup Biscoff creamy cookie spread
- 3/4 cup confectioners' sugar
- 2 cartons (8 ounces each) frozen whipped topping, thawed, divided
- 2 graham cracker crusts (9 inches)
- 1/4 cup caramel sundae syrup
- 4 Biscoff cookies, crushed

Directions

1. Then in a large bowl, beat cream cheese, cookie spread and confectioners' sugar until combined. Fold in 1 carton whipped topping. Divide mixture between crusts. Top with remaining container whipped topping. Drizzle with syrup; sprinkle with cookie crumbs. Freeze, covered, until firm, at least 4 hours.

8. Keto Purple-Ribbon Pumpkin Cake

Prep: 25 min. Bake: 55 min. + cooling | Makes:

12 servings

Ingredients

- 1 can (15 ounces) strong pack pumpkin
- 2 cups sugar
- 4 enormous eggs
- 1 cup vegetable oil
- 2 cups all-purpose flour
- 2 teaspoons heating pop
- 2 teaspoons ground cinnamon
- 1 teaspoon ground cloves
- 1/2 teaspoon salt
- 1/2 teaspoon ground ginger
- 1/4 teaspoon ground nutmeg

CREAM CHEESE FROSTING:

- 2 bundles (3 ounces each) cream cheddar, mollified
- 2 cups confectioners' sugar
- 1 teaspoon vanilla concentrate
- Chopped walnuts, discretionary

Directions

1. In an enormous bowl, beat the pumpkin, sugar, eggs and oil until all around mixed. Join the flour, heating pop, cinnamon, cloves, salt, ginger and nutmeg; gradually beat into pumpkin combination until mixed.
2. Fill a lubed and floured 10-in. fluted tube dish. Prepare at 350° for 55-65 minutes or until cake springs back when gently contacted. Cool for 10 minutes prior to eliminating from dish to a wire rack to cool totally.
3. In a small bowl, beat cream cheddar until cushy. Add confectioners' sugar and vanilla; beat until smooth. Glaze cake; decorate with walnut whenever wanted.

9.   Keto Starbucks Cranberry Bliss Bar

Preparation Time: 10-Mins | Cooking Time: 6-Mins | Serving: 3

INGREDIENTS:

- 1 1/2 sticks of salted butter, cut into cubes
- 1 1/2 cups of brown sugar, packed
- 2-large eggs
- 3/4 teaspoon vanilla extract
- 2 1/4 cups all-purpose flour
- 1 1/2 teaspoons of baking powder
- 1/4 teaspoon of salt
- 1/8 teaspoon of cinnamon
- 1/4 cup dried cranberries, roughly chopped
- 6-ounces baked white chocolate, coarsely chopped frosting:

- 1-pack, 250 ml cream cheese, softened
- 1-cup of powdered sugar
- 10 grams of white baked chocolate, melted
- 1/2 cup dried cranberries, chopped

DIRECTIONS:

1. Oven preheats to 350 degrees F. Sprinkle a 9x13 baking dish with cooking spray. Set aside.

2. Blondie: In a large bowl of brown sugar, they put the melted butter. Mix and let cool to room temperature for about 15 minutes. Scoop butter/sugar aggregate into the mixer/food processor with the paddle attachment.

3. Remove espresso and eggs, combine until miles processed. Watch the flour, saute, and cinnamon together in a medium bowl. Apply the dry elements to the wet gradually. Mix until just absorbed.

4. Stir in the white chocolate and cranberries. The batter will become thick; that is all right.

5. Divide the batter combination into the prepared baking dish. Bake until a toothpick inserted into the center comes out easily for 28-30 minutes. (Make sure you don't overcook. You don't need dry blondie bars.)

6. Place them on a wire rack and let cool.

7. Frosting: Beat the cream cheese and icing sugar together in your stand mixer or hand mixer until well blended. Add half of the melted white chocolate and comb.

8. Divide evenly among blondes. Sprinkle cranberries over the final white chocolate and drizzle.

9. Let the bars cool until cooked and cut into triangles. Keep in the refrigerator until ready to serve. We keep it in the refrigerator for 2-4 days. Love! To enjoy!

10. Coconut Key Lime Pie With Coconut Milk

Prep Time: 10 min| Cook Time: 20 min |Total Time: 30 min | 3 servings

Ingredients

Pie Shell:

- ¼ cup margarine softened
- ½ cup almond flour
- 2 eggs
- ¼ cup low carb sugar substitute or identical sugar
- ¼ teaspoon salt
- ½ cup coconut flour filtered

Filling:

- ¾ cup coconut milk
- ¼ cup weighty cream
- ½ teaspoon priest organic product fluid concentrate or ½ granular sugar

- 2 teaspoons thickener
- 1 teaspoon guar gum or extra thickener
- 3 large egg yolks
- ½ cup Key West Lime Juice
- 2 tablespoons unsweetened shredded coconut optional

Guidelines

Pie Shell:

1. Soften spread in a medium microwavable bowl.

2. Add almond flour, eggs, sugar and salt. Blend well. Mix in filtered coconut flour.

3. Ply mixture with hands for around one moment, at that point shape batter into a ball.

4. Carry out between wax paper to about ⅛ inch think and transform batter into 9 inch pie container.

5. Prick base and sides of outside with fork (if using for a no-prepare filling). Spot a pie safeguard or aluminum foil over the edges to forestall consuming.

6. There's no compelling reason to pre-heat the outside for a prepared pie filling like this

coconut key lime. For a no-heat filling, prepare outside layer at 400°F for 10 minutes (if using for a no-heat filling).

Filling:

1. Join coconut milk, hefty cream, thickener, guar gum and sugar in a food processor or blending bowl.

2. Add egg yolks and lime juice. With food processor edge or electric blender join all ingredients until all around mixed. Mix in dried coconut if using.

3. Spread filling into pie outside.

4. Prepare at 350°F for 10 minutes. Whenever wanted, the pie can be heated for as long as 25 minutes if the middle is too jiggly.

5. Permit to cool for 10 minutes prior to refrigerating. Not long prior to serving, top with whipped cream.

11. Keto Cupcakes - Low Carb, Dairy-Free, Gluten-Free

INGREDIENTS

-
  - cupcakes
  - 2 cups of almond flour
  - 2/3 cup of dark cocoa
  - 1/3 cup of coconut flour
  - 1/3 cup of egg white protein powder
  - 1 tbsp instant coffee optional, enhances the chocolate flavor
  - 1 tbsp baking powder
  - 1/2 teaspoon of salt
  - 1/3 cup of coconut oil
  - 3/4 cup Swerve Sweetener
  - 4-large eggs at room temperature

- 1-teaspoon of vanilla extract
- 3/4 cup unsweetened almond milk
- Cream filling
- 1 13.5 oz can keep full-fat coconut milk refrigerated overnight
- 5 tbsp powdered Swerve Sweetener divided use
- 1/2 teaspoon vanilla extract
- Chocolate Ganache:
- 2 1/2 tbsp Kelapo coconut oil
- 2 ounces of unsweetened chocolate
- 3 tbsp powdered Swerve Sweetener
- 2 tbsp cocoa powder

DIRECTIONS

1. Preheat the oven to 325 ° F and line 15 muffin tins with paper liners (parchment paper is best not to stick). I realize this is an awkward number of cupcakes, but that's how the recipe came out! I did my last three after the first 12 baked.

2. In a medium bowl, whisk almond flour, cocoa powder, coconut flour, meringue powder, instant coffee, baking powder, and salt.

3. In a large bowl, beat coconut oil with sweetener until well blended. Beat in the eggs and vanilla extract.

4. Beat in half of the almond flour mixture and then the almond milk. Beat in the remaining almond flour mixture until well blended.

5. Fill each muffin cup about 2/3 full and bake for 18 to 22 minutes, until just set and a tester in the center comes out clean.

6. Remove from pan and cool in the pan for 10 minutes, then transfer to a wire rack to cool completely.

7. Use a knife or a 1-inch round cookie cutter to cut each cupcake out of the core and cut only the top of each core (to place back on the filled cupcakes).

8. Cream filling

9. Remove the can of coconut milk from the refrigerator and turn it upside down. Open the can and pour out all the coconut water (reserve for smoothies or other uses).

10. Scoop out all of the coconut cream and place in a large bowl.

11. Add 3-tablespoons of powdered sweetener and vanilla extract and beat until i resembles whipped cream.

12. Spoon the filling into the center of each cupcake and cover with a thin top o cupcake cores. You have some leftover cream filling, and use some of it for the white squiggles on the top.

13. Place cupcakes in the fridge while you prepare the ganache.

14. Chocolate Ganache

15. Melt coconut oil, chocolate, and sweetener in a small saucepan over low heat and stir until smooth. Stir in the cocoa powder until smooth.

16. Let sit for 20 to 30 minutes until thick (but don't let it cool completely, or it will be too hard - you want it thick enough to spread over the top of the cakes).

17. Remove the cupcakes from the refrigerator and use a spoon to spread ganache over each of the cupcakes. Cool until set.

18. For the white writing on top, mix 2-tablespoons of the leftover coconut cream

filling with the remaining 2-tablespoons of powdered Swerve until smooth.

19. Spoon into a plastic bag with the tip cut off and pipe on chilled cupcakes of any design

12. High-Protein Muffin Recipe For Busy Mornings

INGREDIENTS:

- Two eggs
- 2 cups of oats
- Two scoops of protein powder
- 1 cup of plain Greek yogurt
- 2/3 cup of milk
- 2 tbsp sugar
- 1 1/2 teaspoons baking powder
- 1/2 teaspoon of baking powder
- 1/2 teaspoon of salt

- One teaspoon of cinnamon
- Blueberries

DIRECTIONS:

1. Preheat the oven to 350 degrees.
2. Mix the eggs, oats, Greek yogurt, and milk in a powerful blender.
3. Pour the mixture into a bowl and mix the rest of the except the blueberries.
4. Spoon the muffin mixture into a greased or parchment-lined muffin tin. Cover the muffins with some blueberries,
5. Bake for 20 minutes.

13. Keto Copycat Chocolate Crunch Bars (Paleo, Vegan, Low Carb)

INGREDIENTS

- 1 1/2 cups chocolate chips of my choice I used stevia sweetened keto-friendly chocolate chips
- 1 cup of almond butter Can be used with any nut or seed butter of your choice
- 1/2 cup of sticky sweetener of your choice
- 1/4 cup of coconut oil
- 3-cups nuts and seeds of your choice almonds, cashews, pepitas, etc.

DIRECTIONS

1. Line a 20 x 20 cm baking dish with baking paper and set it aside.

2. In a microwave-safe bowl or stovetop, combine your choice of chocolate chips, almond butter, sticky sweetener, and coconut oil and melt until combined.

3. Add your nuts/seeds of your choice and mix until completely combined. Pour the keto crunch bar mixture into the parchment-lined baking dish and spread with a spatula. Refrigerate or freeze until set.

14. Chocolate Bread Pudding

Preparation Time: 10-Mins | Serving: 2

INGREDIENTS

-
    - For the chocolate bread pudding
    - 3-cups of cream or milk cream
    - 1-cup of whole milk
    - ½ cup of sugar
    - 300 g chocolate chips
    - 8-egg yolks
    - 2-eggs
    - 1-baguette 500 g
    - For the chocolate sauce
    - 1-cup of cream

- 250 g chocolate chips

DIRECTIONS:

1. Brush a 22 x 33 cm baking tray with butter—Preheat the oven to 180 ° C.
2. Combine the cream, milk, and sugar in a saucepan and simmer, stirring until the sugar dissolves.
3. Remove the pan from the heat. Add the chocolate chips and beat until melted.
4. Beat the egg yolks in a bowl.
5. Gradually add the cream mixture and heat chocolate. Add the inch-square-shaped bread and stir until nicely coated. Let stand for 5 minutes until the dough is cooked.
6. Transfer the bread mixture to the prepared tray.
7. Cover with foil and bake for forty-five minutes. Remove the foil and bake for 15 minutes or until the chocolate bread pudding is cooked. Let cool on a rack.
8. Boil a cup of cream in a small saucepan. Remove from heat and upload the closing

cups of chocolate chips and beat until melted and the chocolate sauce is smooth.

9. Serve the chocolate bread pudding with hot chocolate sauce and crimson fruits.

15. Keto Chocolate Cake Recipe

INGREDIENTS

- For the masses
- 300 g vanilla cookies
- 70 g butter
- For the filling
- 120 g bitter cocoa powder
- 25 cc of milk
- 1-tablespoon of cornstarch
- 6-sachets of sweetener
- 20 g gelatin without hydrated flavor
- 300 g light cream or light cream
- 4-sachets of sweetener

DIRECTIONS:

1. Place the vanilla cookies in a food processor and mash them together with the melted butter. Mix both ingredients well and put them over the bottom of a removable mold. At some point, divide well over the bottom and sides and bake for 5 minutes at 180 ° C.

2. For the chocolate filling, put the milk in a jar with the bitter cocoa powder and mix with a whisk to a bureaucratic cream. Add the cornstarch dissolved in water and mix until included.

3. Remove from heat and upload the sweetener pouches and the unflavored gelatin previously hydrated in water for 10 minutes and dissolved in the microwave for one minute.

4. Integrate thoroughly and reserve. Place the cream or liquid cream in a bowl with the sweetener and beat until semi-hard. Add the chocolate cream while stirring with the spatula until it is sufficiently incorporated and pour over the dough.

16. Keto Copycat Peanut Butter Cheesecake

INGREDIENTS

- 700 g cream cheese
- 2-cups of melted peanut butter
- 1 ½ cup of chocolate chips
- 1½ cup of sugar 1 cup of powdered sugar
- 7-tablespoons of melted butter
- 10-whole wheat cookies
- 1-teaspoon of vanilla extract

DIRECTIONS:

1. Place the whole wheat cookies in a plastic bag and weigh them with a rolling pin.
2. Then put the crumbs in a large bowl and add the melted butter. Mix well into a kind and sandblasted.

3. Place the sandblast in a refractory mold and compact the biscuits. Keep in the fridge.
4. In a large bowl, beat the cream cheese until smooth and add the sugar and vanilla extract. Constantly mix until there are no lumps. Add the melted chocolate and mix until smooth.
5. Pass the idea of biscuits and reserve.
6. In another bowl, mix the melted peanut butter with the icing sugar.
7. Pour this exercise over the previous aggregate and form an even layer using a utility knife to clean the top. Place the peanut butter cheesecake in the fridge for four hours.

17. Pumpkin-Chocolate Chip Pancakes

Yield: It Makes Twelve 4-In Pancakes |Mixing Time: 10 Minutes |Cooking: 4½ To 6 Minutes Per Batch

INGREDIENTS:

- 1 cup unbleached all-purpose flour

- 1 tsp baking powder

- ½ tsp baking soda

- ¼ tsp kosher salt

- 1 tsp. ground cinnamon

- ½ tsp. ground ginger

- ¾ cup milk, any fat content

- one large egg

- 3 tbsp. pure maple syrup

- ¾ cup canned pumpkin

- ¼ cup full-fat or low-fat plain yogurt

- cup semisweet chocolate chips

- 2 tbsp. unsalted butter

- 1 cup vanilla yogurt for serving

DIRECTIONS:

1. Sift the baking powder, flour, baking soda, salt, cinnamon, and ginger into a medium bowl. Add the milk, egg, maple syrup, pumpkin, and plain yogurt. Stir the batter until blended, and there is no loose flour. You may see some small lumps; that's okay. Stir in the chocolate chips just until evenly distributed.

2. Preheat the oven to 250° F. You will be keeping the first batches of pancakes warm in the oven until all the batter is used.

3. Heat a pan, and add 1 tbsp of the butter. Using a pastry brush (preferably silicone), spread the butter evenly over the surface. Using 3 tbsp for each pancake, scoop the batter onto the hot griddle, being careful not to crowd the

pancakes. After 3 to 4 minutes, when bubbles have formed near the pancakes' edges (they will not bubble in the center), the edges have begun to look dry, and the underside is golden brown; carefully turn the pancakes with a spatula.

4. Transfer to a platter and place in the oven. Do not cover the pancakes or they will become get soggy. Repeat with the remaining batter, adding additional butter to the skillet as needed.

5. Serve the pancakes hot and pass the vanilla yogurt at the table.

18. Blueberry Muffins

YIELD: Makes six muffins |MIXING TIME: 5 minutes |REFRIGERATOR TIME: 10 minutes to 2 hours |BAKING: 425°F for about 45 minutes, plus 10 minutes resting time in the oven

INGREDIENTS:

- Flavorless nonstick cooking spray for muffin wells

- three large eggs

- 1½ cups milk, any fat content

- ¾ tsp. kosher salt

- 1½ cups unbleached all-purpose flour

- Butter and jam or Blueberry Sauce for serving

DIRECTIONS:

1. Have ready a rimmed baking sheet. Generously spray six wells in a jumbo muffin tin (or use one of the alternative baking containers suggested in the introductory note) with flavorless nonstick cooking spray.

2. In a bowl, whisk the milk, eggs, and salt until blended. Slowly whisk in the flour just until incorporated. The batter will have small lumps of flour but no large globs. Tap the whisk lightly on the side of the bowl if the flour clumps in the wires.

3. The prepared muffin tin on the baking sheet. Using a scant ½ cup batter for each popover, pour the batter into the prepared wells. The batter should be at least ¼ in from the rim of each well.

4. Turn on the oven to 425°F. Bake until the tops and exposed edges are browned, about 45 minutes. The popovers will rise high over the tops of the cups. Turn off the oven. Using a toothpick, puncture the risen sides in each popover in three places, and let the popovers

sit in the turned-off oven with the oven door closed for 10 minutes. This releases some of the steam in the popovers.

5. Remove as many popovers as needed for a first serving, and leave the remaining ones in the oven for up to 30 minutes to keep warm. Serve with butter and jam.

19. Keto Orange Dream Angel Food Cake

Prep: 25 min. Bake: 30 min. + cooling | Makes: 16 servings

Ingredients

- 12 enormous egg whites
- 1 cup all-purpose flour
- 1-3/4 cups sugar, partitioned
- 1-1/2 teaspoons cream of tartar
- 1/2 teaspoon salt
- 1 teaspoon almond separate
- 1 teaspoon vanilla concentrate
- 1 teaspoon ground orange zing
- 1 teaspoon orange concentrate
- 6 drops red food shading, discretionary
- 6 drops yellow food shading, discretionary

Directions

1. Spot egg whites in a huge bowl; let remain at room temperature for 30 minutes. Filter flour and 3/4 cup sugar together twice; put in a safe spot.

2. Add the cream of tartar, salt and almond and vanilla concentrates to egg whites; beat on medium speed until delicate pinnacles structure. Gradually add remaining sugar, around 2 tablespoons all at once, beating on high until hardened reflexive pinnacles structure and sugar is disintegrated. Gradually overlay in flour blend, around 1/2 cup at a time.

3. Tenderly spoon half of player into an ungreased 10-in. tube container. To the leftover hitter, mix in the orange zing, orange concentrate and, whenever wanted, food colorings. Delicately spoon orange player over white hitter. Slice through the two layers with a blade to twirl the orange and eliminate air pockets.

4. Heat on the least oven rack at 375° for 30-35 minutes or until softly browned and whole top seems dry. Quickly alter dish; cool totally, around 60 minutes.

5. Run a blade around side and focus container of skillet. Eliminate cake to a serving plate.

20. Makeover Traditional Cheesecake

Prep: 40 min. Bake: 1-1/2 hours + chilling |
Makes: 16 servings

Ingredients

- 1-3/4 cups graham wafer pieces
- 2 tablespoons confectioners' sugar
- 1/4 cup margarine, dissolved

FILLING:

- 1 tablespoon lemon juice
- 1 tablespoon vanilla concentrate
- 2 cups 1% curds
- 2 cups decreased fat acrid cream, separated

- 2 bundles (8 ounces each) diminished fat cream cheddar
- 1-1/4 cups sugar
- 2 tablespoons all-purpose flour
- 4 huge eggs, delicately beaten
- 1 tablespoon without fat caramel frozen yogurt besting
- 2 Heath pieces of candy (1.4 ounces each), chopped

Directions

1. Spot a 9-in. springform dish covered with cooking shower on a twofold thickness of hard core foil (around 18 in. square). Safely fold foil over skillet.
2. In a small bowl, consolidate graham wafer morsels and confectioners' sugar; mix in spread. Press onto the base and 1 in. up the sides of arranged skillet. Spot on a heating sheet. Heat at 325° for 18-22 minutes or until daintily browned. Cool on a wire rack.
3. Spot the lemon juice, vanilla, curds and 1 cup sharp cream in a blender; cover and cycle for 2 minutes or until smooth.
4. In an enormous bowl, beat cream cheddar and sugar until smooth. Beat in the excess harsh cream. Add flour and pureed curds combination; blend well. Add eggs; beat on low speed just until consolidated. Fill outside layer.
5. Spot springform dish in a bigger preparing skillet; add 3/4 in. boiling water to bigger

skillet. Heat at 325° for 1-1/2 hours or until focus is simply set and top seems dull. Eliminate springform container from water shower. Cool on a wire rack for 10 minutes.

6. Deliberately run a blade around edge of skillet to slacken; cool 1 hour longer. Refrigerate for the time being. Eliminate sides of container. Trimming with caramel garnish and chopped sweets.

21. Creamy Lemon Pancakes

***YIELD: Makes one pancake |MIXING TIME: 10
minutes |BAKING: 375°F for about 50 minutes
INGREDIENTS:***

- 1 tbsp. unsalted butter

- 2 cups chopped leeks

- 2 cups unbleached all-purpose flour

- ½ tsp. Baking soda

- ½ tsp. Baking powder

- ½ tsp. kosher salt

- Four large eggs

- ½ cups sour cream

- 1 tbsp. grated lemon zest

- ½ tsp. freshly ground black pepper

DIRECTIONS:

1. Preheat the oven to 375°F. Butter a 9-by-5-by-3-in loaf pan (or any loaf pan with an 8-cup capacity).

2. In a frying pan, melt the butter. Add the leeks and cook, often stirring, until softened, about 5 minutes. Remove from the heat.

3. In a medium bowl, stir together the flour, baking soda, baking powder, and salt. Set aside.

4. In a bowl, whisk the eggs. Using a large spoon, stir in the sour cream, leeks with any pan liquid, lemon zest, and pepper. Add the flour and stir, and a sticky dough forms. Scrape the dough into the prepared pan.

5. Bake until the top feels firm and is golden brown, about 50 minutes. Let cool completely before serving.

6. It is good toasted or cooked with a filling in a Panini grill.

22. Keto Donuts with a Rich Chocolate Glaze

Prep Time: 15 min | Cook Time: 15 min |Rest
time: 50 min | Total Time: 30 min

INGREDIENTS

Doughnuts:

- Nonstick oil for container
- 4 large eggs
- ½ cup unsalted margarine liquefied (112 grams)
- 3 tablespoons entire milk
- 1 teaspoon stevia glycerite (approaches ⅓ cup sugar)
- ¼ cup coconut flour

- ¼ cup unsweetened common cocoa powder (not treated with alkali)
- ¼ teaspoon ocean salt
- ¼ teaspoon preparing pop

Coating:

- ¾ cup dull chocolate chips (4.5 oz)
- 1 tablespoon avocado oil

Guidelines

1. Preheat oven to 350 degrees F. Oil 10 silicone doughnut container depressions.
2. Whisk together the eggs, liquefied margarine, milk and stevia.
3. Speed in the coconut flour, cocoa powder, salt and heating pop.
4. Fill the doughnut skillet depressions ¾ full. Heat until set and a toothpick embedded in doughnuts confesses all, around 17 minutes.
5. Spot the container on a cooling rack and permit to cool for 15 minutes.
6. In the mean time, in a shallow bowl, soften the chocolate contributes the microwave, in 30-second spans, blending after every meeting. Mix in the avocado oil.
7. Tenderly run a blade around the edges and focus of every doughnut. Cautiously discharge the doughnuts from the container. Plunge every doughnut into the frosting.

8. Whenever wanted, sprinkle the doughnuts with garnishes like shredded coconut or chopped nuts, or shower with softened peanut butter.

23. Toasted Chocobutter Delight

YIELD: Makes six |MIXING TIME: 10 minutes

BAKING: 400°F for about 18 minutes

INGREDIENTS:

- 2 cups unbleached all-purpose flour

- ¼ cup granulated sugar

- 1¼ tsp. Baking powder

- ¼ tsp. Baking soda

- ¼ tsp. kosher salt

- ½ cup cold butter,

- cup buttermilk, any fat content

- 2 tbsp. pure maple syrup

- 3 oz. semisweet chocolate, chopped

- ½ cup pecans, toasted, and coarsely chopped

- one large egg

- 1 tbsp. heavy cream for egg wash

- Vanilla whipped cream for serving (optional

DIRECTIONS:

1. Preheat the oven to 400°F. Line a baking sheet with parchment paper.

2. In a bowl, whisk the flour, sugar, baking soda, and salt. Scatter the butter pieces over the top. Using your thumb and fingertips, two table knives, or a pastry blender, work the butter into the flour mixture until flour-coated pea-sized pieces form. There will still be some loose flour. Pour the buttermilk and maple syrup into the well, and use a large spoon to mix them into the dry to form a soft dough. Stir in the chocolate and pecans.

3. With floured hands, gather up the dough and put it on a lightly floured work surface. Knead the dough about five strokes: push down and

away with the heel of your hand against the surface, then fold the dough in half toward you, and rotate it a quarter turn, flouring the surface as necessary to prevent sticking. Lightly flour the work surface again and pat the dough into a 7-in circle 1¼ in thick. transfer the scones to the dish

4. Bake till browned, and the bottoms are browned for about 18 minutes. Transfer to a wire rack to cool for at least 15 minutes before serving. Accompany with whipped cream, if desired.

5. The scones can be baked one day ahead, covered, and stored.

24. Keto Chocolate Chiffon Cake

Prep: 25 min. + cooling Bake: 1 hour + cooling | Makes: 20 servings

Ingredients

- 7 enormous eggs, isolated
- 1/2 cup heating cocoa
- 3/4 cup bubbling water
- 1-3/4 cups cake flour
- 1-3/4 cups sugar
- 1-1/2 teaspoons heating pop
- 1 teaspoon salt
- 1/2 cup canola oil
- 2 teaspoons vanilla concentrate

- 1/4 teaspoon cream of tartar
- ICING:
- 1/3 cup margarine
- 2 cups confectioners' sugar
- 2 ounces unsweetened chocolate, liquefied and cooled
- 1-1/2 teaspoons vanilla concentrate
- 3 to 4 tablespoons high temp water
- Chopped nuts, discretionary

Directions

1. Allow eggs to remain at room temperature for 30 minutes. In a bowl, join cocoa and water until smooth; cool for 20 minutes. In an enormous bowl, join flour, sugar, heating pop and salt. In a bowl, whisk the egg yolks, oil and vanilla; add to dry ingredients alongside the cocoa blend. Beat until all around mixed. In another enormous bowl and with clean mixers, beat egg whites and cream of tartar on high velocity until hardened pinnacles structure. Gradually overlay into egg yolk blend.

2. Then delicately spoon hitter into an ungreased 10-in tube skillet. Slice through the player with a blade to eliminate air pockets. Heat on most reduced rack at 325° for 60-65 minutes or until top springs back when gently contacted. Quickly modify skillet; cool totally. Run a blade around sides and focus container of skillet. Rearrange cake onto a serving plate.

3. For icing, dissolve spread in a pan. Eliminate from the heat; mix in the confectioners' sugar, chocolate, vanilla and water. Sprinkle over cake. Sprinkle with nuts whenever wanted

25. Vanilla Wheat Scones

YIELD: Makes six scones |MIXING TIME: 15 mins |BAKING: 350°F for about 15 mins

INGREDIENTS:

- ½ cup cold butter,

- 1 tsp. pure vanilla extract

- ½ tsp. pure almond extract

- ¾ cup buttermilk, any fat content

- ½ cup dried pitted cherries

- 1½ cups unbleached all-purpose flour

- ½ cup whole-wheat flour

- ½ cup granulated sugar, plus 2 tsp.

- 1 tsp. baking powder

- 1 tsp. Baking soda

- ½ tsp. kosher salt

- 1 tsp. ground cinnamon

- 1 tsp. grated orange zest

- One egg

- 3 tbsp. natural or blanched sliced almonds or coarsely chopped natural almonds

- Cherry jam and butter or clotted cream for serving

DIRECTIONS:

1. Preheat the oven to400°F. Line a baking sheet with parchment paper.

2. In a bowl, beat together both flours, the ½ cup sugar, the baking powder, baking soda, salt, and cinnamon. Stir in the orange zest. Scatter the butter pieces over the top. Using your thumb and fingertips, two table knives, or a pastry blender, work the butter into the flour mixture until flour-coated pea-sized pieces form. There will still be some loose flour. Make a well in the center, add the buttermilk, vanilla, almond extract, and cherries to the

well, and mix them into the dry to form a soft dough.

3. Gather the dough into a softball, put it on a floured rolling surface, and pat it into an 8-in circle about ¾ in thick. Cut the circle into eight wedges

4. By cutting it into quarters and then cutting the quarters in half. Use a wide spatula to transfer the scones to the prepared baking sheet, placing them about three apart. Brush the tops with the egg wash. Sprinkle the almonds evenly over the top, pressing them gently onto the dough. Sprinkle the remaining 2 tsp—sugar over the nuts.

5. Bake until the tops are colored, the edges are browned, and the bottoms are browned for about 15 mins. Transfer to cool for at least 15 mins before serving. Accompany with jam and butter.

6. The scones can be baked one day ahead, covered.

26. Hinty Ginger Pancakes

YIELD: Makes 4-in pancakes |MIXING TIME: 10 mins |COOKING: 4½ to 6 mins per batch

INGREDIENTS:

- 3 tbsp. pure maple syrup

- ¾ cup canned pumpkin

- ¼ cup full-fat or low-fat plain yogurt

- cup semisweet chocolate chips

- 2 tbsp. unsalted butter

- 1 cup vanilla yogurt for serving

- 1 cup unbleached all-purpose flour

- 1 tsp. Baking powder

- ½ tsp. Baking soda

- ¼ tsp. kosher salt

- 1 tsp. Ground cinnamon

- ½ tsp. ground ginger

- ¾ cup milk, any fat content

- One egg

DIRECTIONS:

1. Sift the flour, salt, baking powder, cinnamon, and ginger into a bowl. Add the milk, egg, maple syrup, pumpkin, and plain yogurt. Using a spoon, stir the batter until all the are blended, and there is no loose flour. You may see some lumps; that's okay. Stir in the chocolate chips.

2. Preheat the oven to 250° F. You will be keeping the first batches of pancakes warm in the oven until all the batter is used.

3. Heat a griddle or frying pan over heat, and add 1 tbsp of the butter. Using a pastry brush (preferably silicone), spread the butter evenly over the surface. Using 3 tbsp. For each pancake, scoop the batter onto the hot griddle,

being careful not to crowd the pancakes. After 3 to 4 mins, when bubbles have formed near the pancakes' edges (they will not bubble in the center), the edges have begun to look dry, and the underside is golden brown; carefully turn the pancakes with a spatula. Cook until browned, 1½ to 2 mins longer. Shift to a platter in a single layer and place in the oven. Do not cover them. They will become get soggy. Repeat with the remaining batter, adding additional butter to the skillet as needed.

4. Serve the pancakes hot and pass the vanilla yogurt at the table.

27.   Keto baked Cinnamon Rolls

Preparation Time: 15-Mins | Cooking Time: 9-Mins | Serving: 2

INGREDIENTS

- 1 1/2 skewers (12 tablespoons), not listed, softened, more for eating
- 1/3 cup granulated sugar
- 2-possible ground cinnamon
- All-purpose flour for pollinating
- 1-batch like Sweet-Roll Dough, follow up below
- 1 1/4 cups confectioners' sugar
- 4-tablespoons unsalted butter, melted
- 3-tablespoons of milk
- 1/2 teaspoon vanilla extract

- Pinch of salt
- 1/2 cup whole milk
- 1 1/4 packet active dry yeast (2 1/4 teaspoons)
- 1/4 liter of sugar
- 4-tablespoon are unmatched butter, melted, and slithly chilled, plis more for brusing
- 1-large yolk
- 1 1/2 vanilla extract
- 2 3/4 provides all the flour, plus more for it
- 3/4 seasoning salt
- 1/2 teaspoon freshly grated nutmeg (optional)

DIRECTIONS

1. Make the buns: A 9 to 13-inch baking dish. Watch the word and find out in a bowl. On a smooth surface, roll the dough straight out in a 10-by-18-of-inch rectach. Cut the back of the dough, leaving a 1-ish edge on one of the long pieces. Join in with the cinnamon sugar—Fizzy the rest with water. Tight job in an 18-year-old, rolling to the clean border; squeeze the signal to see.

2. Slide an elongated taut piece of thread or unflavored dental floss under the roll about 1 inch from the end. Lift the ends of the wire and move across the roll, pulling firmly to cut a piece. Repeat, cutting every 1-half-inch to make 12 rolls. Place the sandwiches in the organized baking dish.

3. Usually, treat the results with a quick wring and let them go up through heat that doubles in about 1 hour and 10 minutes.

4. Preheat the oven to 350 degrees F. Uncover the buns and bake until they pop down while pressed, 25 to 30 minutes. Only leave in the pan for 10 minutes. (You can release the baked rolls for up to 2 weeks. Be sure to cool before serving.)

5. Make the icing: while you see the item just found, it will be thick, thin, thick, and in a bowl as little as possible. Drizzle over the fun and cozy roles.

6. Heat half a cup of water and milk in a saucepan over low heat until a thermometer registers one hundred degrees F to one hundred- and ten-degrees F. set aside, undisturbed, until me, about 5 minutes.

7. Beat the mixed butter, add some and vanilla in the single combination until combined. In a large bowl, add the flour, sugar, egg, and nutmeg.

8. Make a well in the center, then upload the yeast combination and stir with a wooden spoon to get an idea and beat a bit. Put out a blotchy surface and knead it until slightly and elastic, about 6 minutes. Form into a ball.

9. Brush a large bowl with butter. Add the dough and turn it gently with the butter. Cover with plastic wrap and let rise at room temperature until the mixture has doubled in about 1 hour and 15 minutes.

10. Change the pot's work and flash briefly to the last examples; resume a ball and go back to the ball. At least, but a lot of the first time writing and leaving it on the dough floor. Cover the container and plastic wrap and store in the refrigerator for at least 4 hours or completely in the refrigerator.

28. Keto baked Cheesecake Baileys

Preparation Time: 14-Mins | Cooking Time: 5-Mins | Serving: 7

INGREDIENTS

-
-   For the crust
-   26 Oreo cookies
-   4-tablespoons melted butter Pinch of salt
-   For cheesecake
-   1 kilo of cream cheese
-   1½ cup of regular sugar
-   ¼ cup of cornstarch
-   2/3 cups of Baileys Irish cream
-   1-teaspoon of vanilla extract
-   For the ganache

- 2/3 cups of cream or heavy cream
- 2-cups of chocolate chips

DIRECTIONS:

1. Preheat the oven to 160 ° C and butter a 20 to 23 cm removable mold. Line it with buttered parchment paper too.

2. Mix the Oreo cookies with melted butter and salt. Divide in the tin and set aside while you prepare the filling.

3. In a large bowl, beat the cream cheese and sugar until smooth and fluffy. Add the cornstarch, eggs, vanilla extract, and Irish Cream Baileys.

4. Pour the directions over the crust and place the pan on a sturdy baking tray.

5. Bake the Baileys cheesecake for 80-90 minutes and then let it cool in the oven for 60 minutes. Finally, refrigerate until completely cold for four hours or overnight.

6. When the Baileys Cheesecake is ready to serve, make the Ganache: In a small saucepan, heat the cream or heavy cream over low heat. Place the chocolate chips in a heat-

resistant box and pour the new cream over it
Let stand for three minutes. Then stir unti
there are no more lumps. Chill the ganache fo
15 minutes until thick, then fold it over the
cheesecake. Let stand for 10 minutes and
serve.

29. Keto Chocolate Peanut Butter Cake

Preparation Time: 10-Mins | Cooking Time: 5-Mins | Serving: 2

INGREDIENTS

- 2-cups of wheat flour
- 1-teaspoon of baking powder
- 2-teaspoons of baking powder
- 1/2 teaspoon of salt
- 3/4 cup of natural cocoa powder
- 2-cups of refined sugar
- 2-eggs
- 1/2 cup of vegetable oil
- 1-cup of milk
- 2 1/2 teaspoons vanilla extract
- 1 cup of hot coffee loaded, hot

- 1 cup of creamy peanut butter
- 1/3 cup of sugar glass
- 1-teaspoon unsalted butter softened
- 3-tablespoons of whipped cream
- 2-teaspoons vanilla extract
- Bitumen
- 4 cups of sugar glass
- 1/4 cup unsalted butter
- 1/2 cup of natural cocoa powder
- 1-egg white
- 2-teaspoons vanilla extract
- 1-pinch of salt
- 5-tablespoons of whipped cream

DIRECTION

1. Set the oven to 180ºC (350ºF).
2. Grease and flour 23-centimeter round molds.
3. Sift the flour with baking powder, baking powder, 1/2 teaspoon of salt, and three / four cups of cocoa.
4. Mix the sugar with the oil and the eggs in a large bowl. Add the milk and a few half teaspoons of vanilla; stir well. It contains sifted powders and then hot coffee; Mix until you have a uniform dough. Pour the mixture into the 2-molds and bake for 30 minutes. Remove the desserts from the oven and immediately cover them with foil and cover with a tea

towel. Let cool for 10 minutes. Remove the cakes from the mold and place them on a cord rack. Cover again with the aluminum and cloth (steam keeps them moist). Let them cool down well.

5. Meanwhile, put the filling together. Place the peanut butter, 1/3 cup of sugar glass, and 1-tablespoon of butter. Beat with an electric mixer to a Remar. Add three tablespoons of cream and a few teaspoons of vanilla; mix well. Let stand while the cakes cool.

6. To formulate the bitumen, put 4 cups of glass sugar, 1/4 cup of butter, half a cup of cocoa, egg white, 2-teaspoons of vanilla, a pinch of salt, and five tablespoons of cream in a bowl. Beat with a high-speed electric-powered mixer until you have a creamy bitumen, about 2 minutes. Fill and fill the cold cake.

30. Keto baked Lady Fields Snickerdoodle Cookies

Preparation Time: 10-Mins | Cooking Time: 6-Mins | Serving: 3

INGREDIENTS

- 1/2 cup butter (1 piece, softened)
- 1/2 cup of granulated sugar
- 1/3 cup of brown sugar
- 1-egg
- 1/2 teaspoon vanilla
- 1 1/2 cups of flour
- 1/4 teaspoon of salt
- 1/2 teaspoon of baking powder
- 1/4 teaspoon of cream of tartar

- Cinnamon sugar for rolling:
- 2-tablespoons of granulated sugar
- 1-teaspoon of cinnamon

DIRECTIONS

1. In a large bowl, beat the butter and sugars together with a mixer at high speed. Add the egg and meat and beat until combined.
2. You can put the flour in another bowl, for example, the baking and a piece of butter.
3. Pour the dry elements into most elements and bleed well. Eat dough in the refrigerator for about an hour.
4. After choosing dough, you may have as many as 300 degrees.
5. In no time, integrate the word with the choice for the beginning.
6. Take about 2-variations of the work and make a ball for each choice. Roll it into desired / correct size and place it on a well-laid baking tray. Light a ball slightly with the blade of your hand.
7. Offer them between 12 and 14 minutes and no more. Things will not show up but will be kept

for cooking after being removed from the oven
and left to sit for a while.

31. Keto Chocolate Cake

Preparation Time: 15-Mins | Cooking Time: 9-Mins | Serving: 2

INGREDIENTS

- For the masses
- 300 g vanilla cookies
- 70 g butter
- For the filling
- 120 g bitter cocoa powder
- 25 cc of milk
- 1-tablespoon of cornstarch
- 6-sachets of sweetener
- 20 g gelatin without hydrated flavor
- 300 g light cream or light cream
- 4-sachets of sweetener

- Decorate
- Chocolate without sugar

DIRECTIONS:

1. Place the vanilla cookies in a food processor and mash them together with the melted butter. Mix both ingredients well and put them over the bottom of a removable mold. At some point, divide well over the bottom and sides and bake for 5 minutes at 180 ° C.

2. For the chocolate filling, put the milk in a jar with the bitter cocoa powder and mix with a whisk to a bureaucratic cream. Add the cornstarch dissolved in water and mix until included.

3. Remove from heat and upload the sweetener pouches and the unflavored gelatin previously hydrated in water for 10 minutes and dissolved in the microwave for one minute.

4. Integrate thoroughly and reserve. Place the cream or liquid cream in a bowl with the sweetener and beat until semi-hard. Add the chocolate cream while stirring with the spatula

until it is sufficiently incorporated and pour over the dough.

5. Chill the chocolate cake in the refrigerator for at least 2 hours and grate the unsweetened chocolate.

32. Keto Chocolate Peanut Butter Cake

INGREDIENTS

- 2-cups of wheat flour
- 1-teaspoon of baking powder
- 2-teaspoons of baking powder
- 1/2 teaspoon of salt
- 3/4 cup of natural cocoa powder
- 2-cups of refined sugar
- 2-eggs
- 1/2 cup of vegetable oil
- 1-cup of milk
- 2 1/2 teaspoons vanilla extract
- 1 cup of hot coffee loaded, hot
- 1 cup of creamy peanut butter
- 1/3 cup of sugar glass
- 1-teaspoon unsalted butter softened

- 3-tablespoons of whipped cream
- 2-teaspoons vanilla extract
- 2-teaspoons vanilla extract
- 1-pinch of salt
- 5-tablespoons of whipped cream

DIRECTION

1. Set the oven to 180ºC (350ºF).
2. Grease and flour 23 centimeter round molds.
3. Sift the flour with baking powder, baking powder, 1/2 teaspoon of salt, and three / four cups of cocoa.
4. Mix the sugar with the oil and the eggs in a large bowl. Add the milk and a few half teaspoons of vanilla; stir well. It contains sifted powders and then hot coffee; Mix until you have a uniform dough. Pour the mixture into the 2-molds and bake for 30 minutes. Remove the desserts from the oven and immediately cover them with foil and cover with a tea towel. Let cool for 10 minutes. Remove the cakes from the mold and place them on a cord rack. Cover again with the aluminum and cloth (steam keeps them moist). Let them cool down well.

5. Meanwhile, put the filling together. Place the peanut butter, 1/3 cup of sugar glass, and 1 tablespoon of butter. Beat with an electric mixer to a Remar. Add three tablespoons o cream and a few teaspoons of vanilla; mix well. Let stand while the cakes cool.

33. Keto Recipe For Chinese Almond Cookies

INGREDIENTS

- 2 3/4 cups of wheat flour
- 1-cup of refined sugar
- 1/2 teaspoon of baking powder
- 1/2 teaspoon of salt
- 1 cup of lard
- 1-egg

DIRECTIONS:

1. Before 165 ° C (325 ° F).

2. Sift the flour with sugar, baking powder, and salt into a bowl. Add the butter and upload it with forks until you have a sandy mixture. Add the egg and almond extract; mix well.

3. Form balls with a diameter of 2 centimeters and place them 5 centimeters apart in ungreased baking trays. Place 1-almond on top

of each ball and press with your finger to flatten slightly.

4. Bake at 165 ° C for 15-18 minutes. Place on cooling racks.

Nutritional Information:

- Calories: 285kcal
- Carbohydrates: 7 g
- Protein: 12g
- Fat: 24 g
- Saturated fat: 6 g
- Cholesterol: 155 mg
- Sodium: 187 mg
- Potassium: 131 mg
- Fiber: 6 g
- Sugar: 1 g
- Vitamin A: 550IU
- Calcium: 107 mg
- Iron: 8 mg

34. Keto Chocolate Bread Pudding

INGREDIENTS

- For the bread pudding
- 5-cups of challah or challah bread
- 1 cup of whole milk
- 1 cup of heavy cream
- ¾ cups of chocolate chips
- ½ cup of sugar
- ¼ cup of bitter cocoa powder
- 1-tablespoon of unsalted butter
- 1-teaspoon of cinnamon powder
- ½ teaspoon of salt
- 1-teaspoon of vanilla extract

DIRECTIONS:

1. Cut the bread into small cubes. While you can use fresh food as is, hard bread will absorb drinks much better. If you are using fresh bread, lightly toast the cubes by spreading them out on a baking tray and placing them in the 180 ° C oven for 10 minutes.

2. Combine bitter powder, sugar, salt, floor, cinnamon, heavy cream, whole milk, vanilla extract, and eggs in a large bowl.

3. Preheat oven to 180 ° C. Spread a 10 x 7-inch baking dish with butter and pour in the bread and liquid aggregate.

4. Place the pan on a baking sheet and bake for 40 minutes or until the mixture is set.

5. Cover by melting the chocolate chips in the microwave for several seconds and stirring the cream until smooth. Pour the topping over the chocolate bread pudding and serve warm or at room temperature

35. Two-Berry Pavlova

Prep: 20 min. + standing| Bake: 45 min. + cooling | Makes: 12 servings

Ingredients
- 4 huge egg whites, room temperature
- 1/2 teaspoon cream of tartar
- 1 cup sugar
- 1 tablespoon cornstarch
- 1 teaspoon lemon juice

Fixings:
- 2 cups new blackberries
- 2 cups cut new strawberries
- 1/4 cup in addition to 3 tablespoons sugar, separated
- 1-1/4 cups substantial whipping cream

Directions

1. Spot egg whites in an enormous bowl. Line a heating sheet with material; attract a 10. circle on paper. Transform paper.

2. Preheat oven to 300°. Add cream of tartar to egg whites; beat on medium speed until delicate pinnacles structure. Gradually add sugar, 1 tablespoon at a time, beating on high after every option until sugar is broken down. Keep beating until firm shiny pinnacles structure. Overlay in cornstarch and lemon juice.

3. Spoon meringue onto arranged container; with the rear of a spoon, shape into a 10-in. circle, shaping a shallow well in the middle. Prepare until meringue is set and dry, 45-55 minutes. Mood killer oven (don't open oven entryway); leave meringue in oven 60 minutes. Eliminate from oven; cool totally on preparing sheet.

4. To serve, throw berries with 1/4 cup sugar in a small bowl; let stand 10 minutes. In the mean time, in an enormous bowl, beat cream until it starts to thicken. Add remaining sugar; beat until delicate pinnacles structure.

5. Eliminate meringue from material; place on a serving plate. Spoon whipped cream up and over, framing a slight well in the middle. Top with berries.

36. Blueberries and Cream Coffee Cake

Prep: 20 min. Bake: 55 min. + cooling | Makes: 12 servings

Ingredients

- 1 cup spread, mollified
- 2 cups sugar
- 2 huge eggs, room temperature
- 1 teaspoon vanilla concentrate
- 1-3/4 cups all-purpose flour
- 1 teaspoon preparing powder
- 1/4 teaspoon salt
- 1 cup sharp cream
- 1 cup new or frozen unsweetened blueberries
- 1/2 cup stuffed brown sugar
- 1/2 cup chopped walnuts, discretionary
- 1 teaspoon ground cinnamon
- 1 tablespoon confectioners' sugar

Directions

1. In a huge bowl, cream spread and sugar until light and feathery, 5-7 minutes. Add eggs, 1 al at once, beating admirably after every option. Beat in vanilla. Consolidate the flour, heating powder and salt; add to the creamed combination then again with harsh cream, beating admirably after every option. Crease in blueberries.
2. Spoon half of player into a lubed and floured 10-in. fluted tube dish. In a small bowl, consolidate the brown sugar, walnuts whenever wanted, and cinnamon. Sprinkle half absurd. Top with outstanding player; sprinkle with staying brown sugar blend. Slice through player with a blade to twirl the brown sugar combination.
3. Heat at 350° until a toothpick embedded close to the middle confesses all, 55-an hour. Cool for 10 minutes prior to eliminating from skillet to a wire rack to cool totally. Not long prior to serving, dust with confectioners' sugar.

Nutrition Facts

- 1 slice:
- 428 calories
- 20g fat (12g saturated fat)
- 76mg cholesterol
- 233mg sodium
- 60g carbohydrate (45g sugars, 1g fiber)
- 4g protein.

37. Keto Cream Cheese Brownies

Yield: 9 Brownies Prep Time: 15 Minutes Cook Time: 30 Minutes Total Time: 45 Minutes

Ingredients

- Cream Cheese Filling
- 8 oz cream cheddar, relaxed
- 1 enormous egg
- 1 tsp vanilla
- 1/4 cup powdered erythritol
- Brownies
- 2 Large eggs
- 1/2 cup erythritol, (or brown sugar turn)
- 6 tbsp margarine, unsalted
- 3 oz unsweetened bread cook's chocolate
- 1 tsp vanilla
- 1/4 cup coconut flour

- 1/2 tsp salt
- 1/2 tsp heating powder
- 2 tbsp weighty cream, optional for assist with marbling

Guidelines

1. Preheat oven to 350 and oil a 8x8 dish. Put in a safe spot.
2. In a medium bowl, beat cream cheddar until whipped. Blend in egg, vanilla and powdered erythritol until all around joined. Put in a safe spot.
3. In an enormous bowl, beat eggs until they are foamy. Mix in erythritol and blend well.
4. In a little microwave safe bowl, soften spread and chocolate for 30 second spans blending between heatings, until chocolate is totally dissolved.
5. Add vanilla, salt, heating powder and liquefied chocolate to the bowl with the eggs and mix well.
6. Gradually mix in coconut flour (in 1 tbsp increases works best)

7. When blended, spread 3/4 of the brownie combination into the readied skillet.

8. Spoon the cream cheddar combination on top and smooth it around.

9. Spread the remainder of the brownie combination on top of the cream cheddar blend to make a marbled look. (add 2 tbsp substantial cream prior to adding to assist with marbling)

10. Heat 25-30 minutes or until a toothpick insterted in the middle tells the truth.

Conclusion

I would like to thank you for going through these recipes. These recipes will help you in making delicious desserts at home. As per an investigation done by analysts, keto dessert for breakfast is useful in case that you need to shed pounds. Eating keto dessert is solid and fat individuals should add treat to their eating routine when taking breakfast. Prepare for yourself, your family members and appreciate. Good luck!